When You Came

A Jewish Book of Arrival, Greeting, Celebration

WRITTEN BY

Jennifer Tzivia MacLeod

ILLUSTRATED BY

Hiruni Kariyawasam

When You Came: A Jewish Book of Arrival, Greeting, Celebration

© 2021/5781 Jennifer Tzivia MacLeod

First softbound edition
ISBN-13: 978-1-988976-12-9 (Safer Editions)
ISBN-10: 1-988976-12-X

All Rights Reserved. No part of this publication may be reproduced, stored in a retrieval system, or transmitted, in any form or in any means – by electronic, mechanical, photocopying, recording or otherwise – without prior written permission.

"הַיּוֹם שֶׁבּוֹ נוֹלַדְתְּ,
הוּא הַיּוֹם בּוֹ אֱלֹקִים הֶחֱלִיט
שֶׁהָעוֹלָם אֵינוֹ יָכוֹל לְהִתְקַיֵּם בִּלְעָדַיִךְ"

"The day you were born is the day G-d decided
the world could not exist without you."
(Traditional Jewish saying)

Before you came, we waited for a very long time.

Sometimes, we hardly believed it would happen.

וְזַכֵּנִי לְגַדֵּל בָּנִים וּבְנֵי בָנִים...
May I merit to raise children & grandchildren...
(prayer after Shabbat candle lighting)

אֶל־הַנַּעַר הַזֶּה הִתְפַּלָּלְתִּי וַיִּתֵּן ה' לִי אֶת־שְׁאֵלָתִי...
For this child have I prayed, and G-d has granted me my request...
(I Samuel 1)

We were so excited to meet you.

Wondering what you might look like.

We dreamed and wished and prayed.

When you came, everybody wanted to see you first.

We tried to hug you gently.

As we showed you how amazed we were to meet you at last.

...שֶׁהֶחֱיָנוּ וְקִיְּמָנוּ וְהִגִּיעָנוּ לַזְּמַן הַזֶּה

...שֶׁהֶחֱיָנוּ וְקִיְּמָנוּ וְהִגִּיעָנוּ לַזְּמַן הַזֶּה.
...Who has kept us alive and sustained us and brought us to this day.
(prayer for special occasions)

אוֹדְךָ עַל כִּי נוֹרָאוֹת נִפְלֵיתִי...
I will thank You, for I was fashioned in an awesome, wondrous way ...
(Psalms 139)

Now we knew what we'd been missing all along:

Your toes, your chin, your voice.

On your first Shabbat, we blessed you:

"May you be like…"

Connecting you to ancient generations

with candles and sweet wine and challah

We sang around the table to welcome the angels

Even though we couldn't take our eyes off you.

יברכך ה' וישמרך...

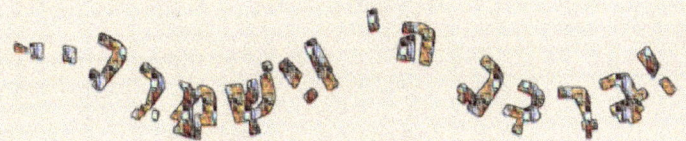

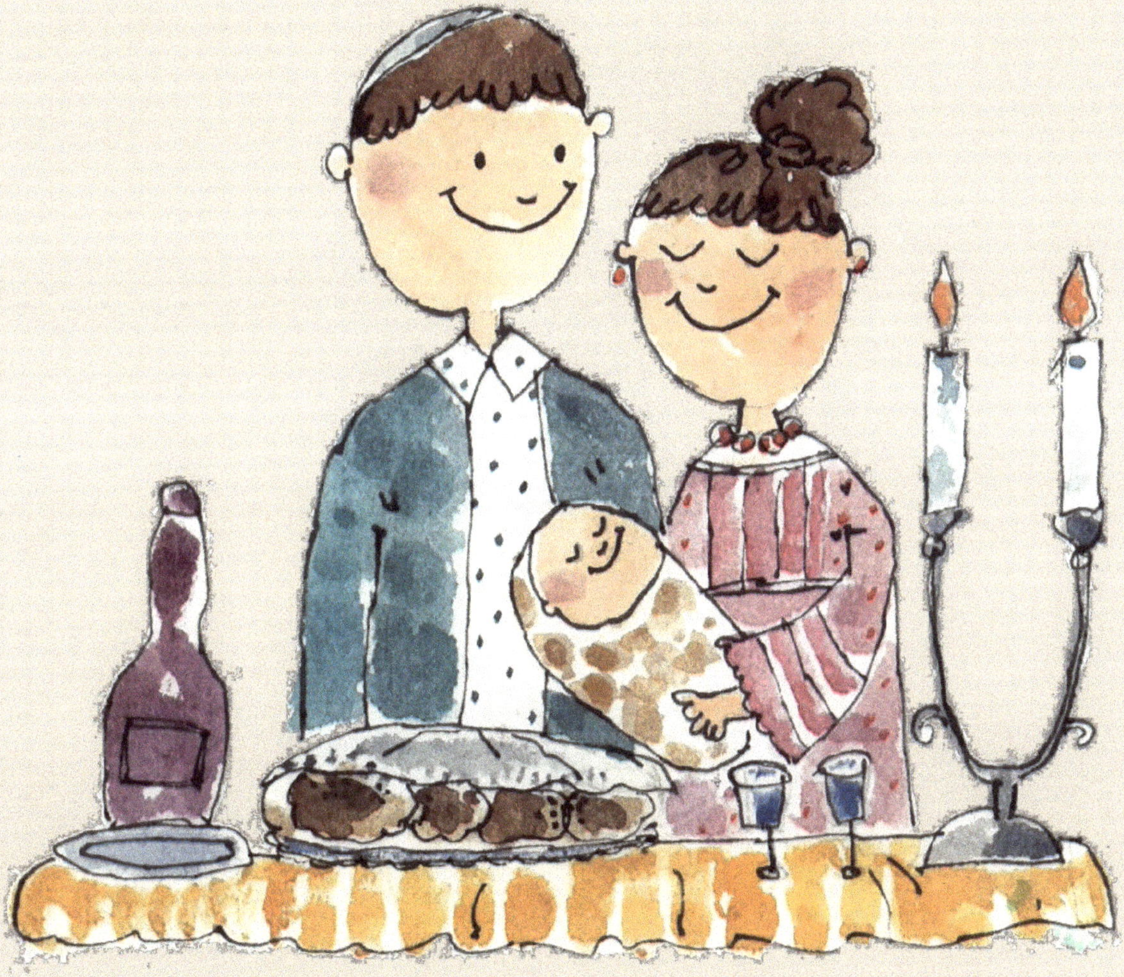

יְבָרֶכְךָ ה' וְיִשְׁמְרֶךָ...

May G-d bless you and keep you...

(Friday-night blessing for children)

מוֹדֶה אֲנִי לְפָנֶיךָ מֶלֶךְ חַי וְקַיָּם...
I am grateful to You, living and enduring King...
(morning blessing)

After you came, mornings were not always easy.

You had ideas and habits all your own

that we all had to learn.

Some afternoons, we prayed for quiet…

But then we couldn't wait to see you again

and hear about your adventures.

ה' יִשְׁמָר צֵאתְךָ וּבוֹאֶךָ מֵעַתָּה וְעַד עוֹלָם:
May G-d guard your going out and your coming in, from now on and forever.
(traveler's prayer, from Psalm 121)

הַמַּלְאָךְ הַגֹּאֵל אֹתִי מִכָּל־רָע יְבָרֵךְ אֶת־הַנְּעָרִים...
May the angel who redeems me from all harm bless the youths...
(bedtime prayer)

Evenings with you were wet and noisy

between bubbles and ducks and Niagara Falls.

Sometimes we were almost too tired

to say Shema at bedtime,

but we said it anyway, just for you.

Late nights were exhausting and teary.

But friends and family brought laughter by day,

surrounding our lives with light and love.

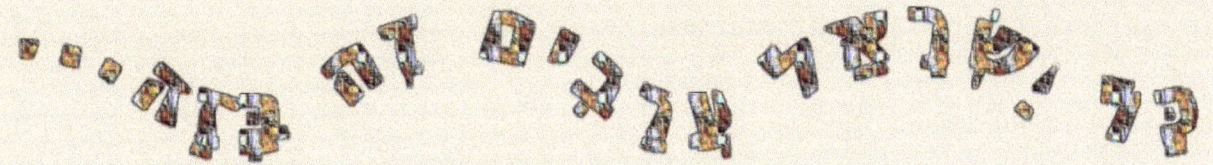

כל ישראל ערבים זה בזה...

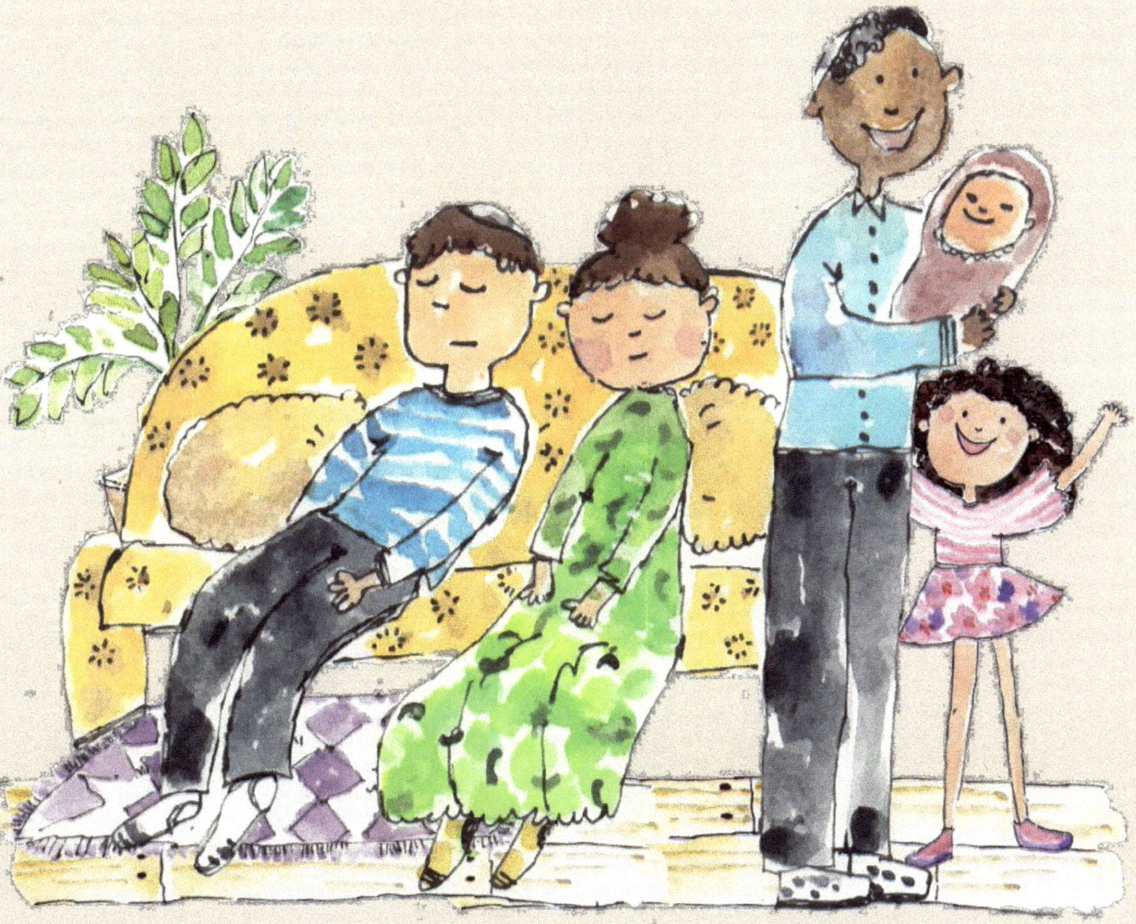

כָּל יִשְׂרָאֵל עֲרֵבִים זֶה בָּזֶה...

All Jews are responsible for one another...

(Talmud)

מַה טֹּבוּ אֹהָלֶיךָ, יַעֲקֹב...
How lovely are your tents, O Jacob...
(prayer on entering the synagogue)

Once you came, we welcomed you to the Jewish people,

joining the family of Abraham and Sarah

with a life of mitzvot ahead.

Your name had to be perfect;

Part of our family, but all your own.

Our community gathered to welcome you,

take you by the hand and start you on your way.

לְתוֹרָה לְחֻפָּה וּלְמַעֲשִׂים טוֹבִים...
[May he or she grow] to Torah, marriage, and good deeds...
(prayer on naming a baby)

שְׁמַע קוֹלֵנוּ ה' אֱלֹקֵינוּ, חוּס וְרַחֵם עָלֵינוּ...
Hear our voice, G-d, have compassion upon us...
(daily prayer)

Before you came,

we dreamed and wished and prayed.

And now that you're here…

We pray

    And dance

        And cry

            And sing

                    Together

שֶׁעוֹלָם אֵינוּ יָכוֹל לְהִתְקַיֵּם בִּלְעָדֶיךָ.

And cannot imagine the world without you in it.

...הָעוֹלָם אֵינוּ יָכוֹל לְהִתְקַיֵּם בִּלְעָדֶיךָ.
The world could not exist without you.

וּרְאֵה בָנִים לְבָנֶיךָ שָׁלוֹם עַל יִשְׂרָאֵל.

The End

וּרְאֵה בָנִים לְבָנֶיךָ שָׁלוֹם עַל יִשְׂרָאֵל.
And may you see children born to your children; peace upon Israel.
(Psalms 128)

Meet the Author & Illustrator

Jennifer Tzivia MacLeod is the proud mother of four kids - two big and two bigger. She lives in northern Israel with her family. The author of more than two dozen books for Jewish kids and families, she is a SCBWI Crystal Kite award winner and has also received PJ Library's Author Incentive Award. Visit her at Tzivia.com

Hiruni Kariyawasam is a hardworking undergraduate student in fashion design. For her children's book illustrations, she draws, paints and digitally manipulates the illustrations, creating a handmade feel along with a sense of curiosity and innocence. Follow her at www.instagram.com/hiru_k96/

If you liked this book, please help us out by taking a minute to leave a review.

Thank you!

You Might Also Enjoy...

More from author Jennifer Tzivia MacLeod:

The Family Torah
Weekly parsha companion for kids & families
http://tinyurl.com/familytorah

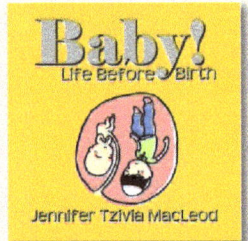

Baby! Life Before Birth
Explore G-d's amazing world by visiting a baby before she's born – along with her excited big brother!
http://tinyurl.com/readbaby

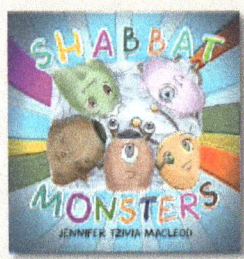

Shabbat Monsters
Shabbat is a sad time for one newcomer who just doesn't fit in. Will the other monsters let him join in the fun?
http://tinyurl.com/ShabbatMonsters

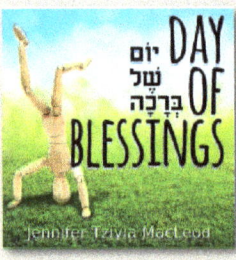

Day of Blessings:
Traditional Jewish Morning Blessings in Rhyme
Share with kids the wonderful blessings that fill our lives every single day in a light, fun way.
http://tinyurl.com/DayofBlessings